SAILING

CORGI BOOKS

THE GOLDEN RULES OF SAILING

A CORGI BOOK 0 552 12594 6

First publication in Great Britain

PRINTING HISTORY
Corgi edition published 1985

Corgi Books are published by Transworld Publishers Ltd.,
Century House, 61-63 Uxbridge Road, Ealing, London W5 5SA,
in Australia by Transworld Publishers (Aust.) Pty. Ltd.,
26 Harley Crescent, Condell Park, NSW 2200, and in New
Zealand by Transworld Publishers (N.Z.) Ltd., Cnr. Moselle
and Waipareira Avenues, Henderson, Auckland.

Made and printed in Great Britain by
Hunt Barnard Printing Ltd., Aylesbury, Bucks.

Buying a boat in kit-form is the cheapest way of obtaining a new boat. The small sailing dinghy is usually very simple to assemble.

It is essential that every yachtsman should be able to row, as sooner or later it will be needed.

A beginner should never attempt to sail when the wind is particularly strong.

Always buy good waterproof clothing and check it as soon as possible.

Take special care when using a trapeze, as it can be a tricky piece of equipment to handle.

Always go to a recognized dealer to buy any type of craft, unless you are buying privately.

When on deck in rough weather it is essential to wear a harness.

Never get into a boat which is on its road trailer.

You must allow for the fall or rise in water when mooring to a jetty, pier or harbour wall.

Be ready to listen to any advice or instructions from any person in authority, especially when you are in unfamiliar surroundings.

Never attempt to sail if you do not feel physically fit, as sailing can be arduous.

Some areas of water are reserved strictly for other uses, such as water-skiing. Make sure you do not stray into these areas.

Make sure that the anchor is not too heavy and that the rope or chain is long enough.

A small auxiliary motor is very useful when trying to manoeuvre in harbours or when a boat is becalmed.

It is advisable to wear practical and comfortable clothes at all times when sailing.

During a race a yacht may be propelled only by the natural actions of wind on the sails, spars and hulls, and water on the hull.

It is important to be able to throw a painter cleanly and accurately.

Putting up a mast can be difficult and it is prudent to have help in doing this.

When transporting a boat by car ensure that it is securely fastened to the roof-rack.

It is important that you learn to read and understand charts.

When gybing or going about remember to keep clear of the boom.

It is advisable for the beginner to have a few lessons with a good sailing school before going out alone.

Remember to undo the spring clip which locks the bottom pintle when taking the rudder off, or else it will not move.

Launching a sailing dinghy should be done in favourable weather conditions and away from any hazards.

Reefing is essential in certain weather conditions and it can also be of benefit to the beginner.

Sailing depends on the wind, so it is necessary to detect its direction prior to, and during, sailing.

It is important to learn and remember as many nautical terms as you can.

Always carry basic safety equipment in the boat at all times.

An obvious fact, but one which should be remembered by the beginner, is that there are no brakes on a boat!

It is unwise for a beginner to contemplate sailing in extreme weather conditions.

Do not panic if you run aground. Attempt to refloat the boat or wait for help to arrive.

Take extreme care when getting into or out of a small boat, as it is easy to cause damage to either yourself or the craft.

Always carry a baler or something similar, in the boat. Ensure that the container is large enough.

Ensure that you know the correct procedure in case of man overboard.

Never sail into or close to sailing dinghies participating in a race if you are not involved.

The most practical way to right a capsized dinghy is to climb on to the centreboard and to pull the boat upright by the jib-sheet.

The centreboard is used to stop the boat slipping sidewards over the water. Ensure you know when to use it and how much to use.

Ensure that your boat is securely moored if not being used, even if only for a short time.

When manoeuvring a boat on land, or to and from the water, always check that you are not near to any overhead cables.

In general, power should give way to sail, but remember that this is NOT a rule.

It is vital to keep alert at all times when sailing.

Hoisting the mainsail is a fairly simple process as long as it is done methodically.

If you are capsized or in dire trouble do everything in your power to alert passing vessels of your position and circumstances.

45

Never overload a sailing dinghy. If it is built to carry only two persons, it is unwise and dangerous to have any more persons aboard.

Above all, never forget that all aspects of sailing are to be enjoyed.